Bovey Tracey Potteries

Guide and Marks

Brian Adams

Curator of The Bovey Tracey Pottery Museum

at House of Marbles

Bovey Tracey Potteries, Guide and Marks

Copyright © Brian Adams, 2005

Published by House of Marbles, Pottery Road, Bovey Tracey, Devon, U.K.   *Telephone*   01626 835285

First published   2005

Acknowledgments

Thanks are due to the many people who have assisted in creating the Bovey Tracey Pottery Museum at House of Marbles. This particular publication has been made possible by the following, who have generously provided information, photographs or access to their collections: -
Garry Atkins, Ken Bond, Adrian Bunclark, George Edwards Carter, George Cattle, Dean Edwards, Valerie Haslam, Martin and Brenda Hicks, Tricia Hope, Les Manley, Rosemary Millman, Pat Purchase, Bob Ross, Keith Taylor, Anthony Thomas, David Thorn, Robin Thornton, Morris Tucker, Liz Westwood, Candy Tiles (1992) Limited, The Royal Albert Memorial Museum, Exeter, Howard Mumford and Friends of Blue.

Printed by Brightsea Press, Clyst Honiton, Exeter, Devon, EX5 2UL

ISBN   0 - 9549744 - 0 - 9

Contents

ottery making has been carried on continuously in the Bovey Tracey area since 1750, when the opening of the local coal pits allowed the commercial exploitation of abundant mineral wealth in this land of clay. Throughout its 250 year history, the local industry has been a microcosm of national trends in pottery making. The effects of the industrial revolution, of national strife and of economic turmoil, have all been reflected in this idyllic corner of countryside Britain.

To the inexperienced eye the pottery of Bovey Tracey is the same as the products of Staffordshire, but there are differences. It is true that these were "Staffordshire" potteries transplanted to a rural County, but being so far from the centre of the industry, it was necessary to become self sufficient. Every pottery trade was carried out locally and Devonshire styles emerged in the products. It is very satisfying to correctly identify the products of Bovey Tracey in the absence of marks, relying on style alone.

An unmarked inkwell from the 1790s was purchased for £5 and is now valued at £300 - £400. Specialist collectors will pay upwards of £2000 for a tea canister from the 1760s. Those of lesser means can acquire interesting and rare decorative dishes from the 1950s for the equivalent of a few shillings. Local interest

can be reflected in collections of inexpensive commemoratives marked with Devon town and village names or in very expensive pots from the 1700s inscribed with local family names. Those who want something distinctive can follow the example of United States President F.D.Roosevelt, who collected Bovey Wemyss pigs just for fun. F.D.R. was also featured as a pottery character in the Bovey Pottery "Our Gang" series, a must for any collector of wartime memorabilia.

There is a wealth of Bovey Tracey pottery, much of it unidentified, awaiting collectors of all financial means and interests in fairs, markets and auction rooms throughout the world - the market with which the potters traded.

These kilns at Bovey Tracey, pictured in 1989 when they were in a state of decay, are among the few remaining conspicuous signs of a once thriving industry. Less obvious such evidence is still to be discovered - in archives, within the memories of local families, and among the pots and relics we preserve as collectables and antiques.

The First Potteries

I n the year 1750, Lord William Courtenay, the Earl of Devon, opened the clay and lignite (brown coal) pit at what is now known as Blue Waters near Bovey Tracey. The new "coal adventure" was immediately exploited by several potters from Staffordshire, now able to use their clay without the need of transporting it the 200 or so miles to their home country. Lord Courtenay, local investors, and adventurers from Cornwall co-operated in these new potteries - but they were not without their problems. Jeremiah Milles, the Dean of Exeter wrote:

> *".... they succeeded tolerably well, but it soon miscarried, either as the Proprietors said, because the workmen were bribed to destroy it, or as the workmen said, because the Bovey coal, which they made use of in burning it, was not of a heat intense enough to answer the purpose."*

The main pottery site was close to the clay and lignite pits at Heathfield. Another pottery was almost certainly working at Pond Garden next to Indeo Pond for a short time.

Remains of a kiln dating from about 1760 were discovered at Fore Street, Bovey Tracey in 1932 along with several unfinished and kiln-damaged saltglazed pots. The kiln remains were moved to The Candy Tile Works at Heathfield. They are soon to be moved to House of Marbles, where they will be open to view.

The organisation of the first potteries seems to have been rather haphazard with several groups working within or on the fringes of Lord Courtenay's enterprise.

Pottery sherds and kiln furniture provide archaeological evidence of saltglazed pottery and tortoiseshell ware production at Heathfield, at Pond Garden and at Fore Street, but no examples have been identified with the early sites. Any complete pots in existence are probably not marked and are likely to be attributed to Staffordshire.

Above. *Cutaway section of the Fore Street kiln, being loaded with pots set in saggars in the 1750s.*

Left *Unfinished and kiln-damaged saltglazed ware dating from about 1760, discovered with the Fore Street kiln in 1932.*

The Indeo Pottery

Nicholas Crisp, a well-known business adventurer, jeweller and potter, moved to Bovey Tracey in 1766, having been declared bankrupt in London. He brought his key workers with him and, with the backing of "a few gentlemen of fortune," established a porcelain and pottery manufactory at Indeo House, seat of Squire George Tuffnell.

A saltglaze Gossiping Cup and a tea canister moulded with the head of Ceres, the Goddess of Plenty, are said to have been the first two pieces drawn from the first kiln fired at Indeo in 1766. The small figure, a mother and baby, is based on a fragment found at the Indio site.

William Cookworthy, the Plymouth chemist, took advantage of Nicholas Crisp's new Indeo Pottery, having many of his porcelain experiments carried out there. Despite this opportunity, Nicholas Crisp was declared bankrupt (yet again) within two years of opening at Bovey, and could not pay his workers. They went on to Plymouth and played an important part in establishing William Cookworthy's porcelain manufactory, which produced the first true porcelain in the British Isles. Nicholas Crisp and his family struggled on at Indeo until he died in 1774.

In the meantime, William Ellis, a young local potter, raised more finance, and in 1772 re-established the Indeo Pottery under his own management. Other local potteries were quickly absorbed into the new Indeo venture, which was carried on under various partnerships for seventy years until 1836, employing up to 45 potters. They continued producing most of the kinds of pottery then being made in Staffordshire.

Josiah Wedgwood of that County visited Indeo in 1775, passing through Devon on his way to Cornwall on his quest to break Cookworthy's porcelain patent. He commented:

> " they.... made white stoneware glazed with Salts, and had a fireman, and I believe some other workmen from our country.... They now make Queen's Ware, or cream-colour, but it is a poor trifling concern, and conducted in a wretched slovenly manner..... having the clay within 5 or 6 miles of them, from the same pitts which furnish our potteries in Staffordshire.... The coals are only 2/6 per ton, at the pit, and so near the works,.... Notwithstanding all which advantages, We can carry their clay and flints from Devonshire into Staffordshire, there manufacture them into ware, and send it back to their own doors better and cheaper than they can make it."

The Indeo Pottery on the day of Wedgwood's visit . He is sitting on the wall. The pottery foreman, Tom Prouse, is working in the foreground, being assisted by his family.

Josiah Wedgwood's comments are often used to discredit the products of the Indeo Pottery, but recent research has shown that, besides some very ordinary, naive and even coarse pottery, some high quality and intricately made wares were also made. Tea canisters inscribed with their owners' names are well known. Examples of Nicholas Crisp's porcelain are among the rarest in existence. The Indeo potters took advantage of the rich diversity of local minerals, experimenting with several new kinds of pottery.

Engine turned and moulded creamware of the 1770s, including f r a g m e n t s excavated at the Indeo Pottery site in the 1990s

INSCRIPTIONS ON INDEO POTTERY

Many of the pots are inscribed with people's names, often commemorating births or marriages.

SALTGLAZE TEA CANISTERS
Inscriptions are scratched by hand and usually coloured blue - "scratch blue."

Mary Coall. Made by Thomas Prouse
-   September ye 26th 1767.

Elizabeth Lamble 1768
Christopher Stonlake 1768
Mary Pugsle 1768
John Allward March ye.17th: 1768
Jane Toper 1769
Ann Heard 1769

M. Hutchings 1769

William Wotton 1769

Ann Lamacrat Sept ye 4th 1770

Martha Saymore September ye 21th 1770

Mrs Medland October ye 8th 1770

Suzanna Savery July ye 19th 1770

M.H. 1769

Elizabeth Steer 1769

Joanna Ellis 1770

Grace Nichols 1770

Ann Surcombe 1770

Ann Cook October ye 8th 1770

SALTGLAZED STONEWARE BOTTLES

The inscriptions are impressed with printer's type. The bottles almost certainly contained the famous Ashburton pop, a potent brew drunk from white saltglaze mugs made at Indeo. The recipe is long lost.

R. Halse Jun. Ashburton 1771

D. Dobell Ashburton 1775

G. Quint Ashburton

CREAMWARE TEA CANISTERS

The inscriptions of the 1770s are mainly scratched and coloured blue or brown. Scratch brown was a speciality of The Indeo Pottery.

Andrew Arnold

Ann Addams 1771

Thos Moore 1771

Sarah Browning 1772

Ann Louden 1772

Prisilia Pearse 1772

Grace Henman 1772

Mary Marten 1772

William Youlton to Sally Pope 1772
Mrs. Mary Chase, Kimberton Oct. 10th 1772
Elizabeth Grills 1773
Frances Breley October 9th 1773
Abraham and Alice Randell 1779

Polly Carder 1773
Jane Smale October 7th 1773
Elizh Halistay 1778 (unclear)
Joan Tavner Novr the 3rd 1787

CREAMWARE FLASKS (not illustrated). James Cook. Dec. ber ye 3th 1771

CREAMWARE INKWELLS

Mary Darges September ye 28th 1771
Miss Mary Adams 1772

Right : *Author's impression*

TEAPOTS, BOWLS AND MUGS

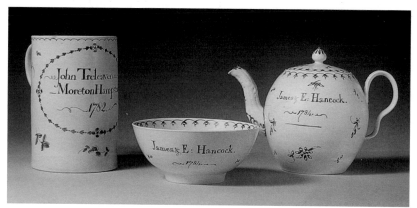

Creamware of the 1780s usually has handpainted inscriptions in blue.

James & E. Hancock 1784
Ann White, Crediton Jany: 22[d] 1781 (teapot)
George Lacey born January 6th. 1781 (mug)
John Treleaven, MORETON HAMPSTEAD 1782 (mugs)

CREAMWARE JUG
Wm. Kingwell 1782

OTHER CREAMWARE
"Barrett Tap-house"
(on a sherd found at Indeo.)

KETTLES   Eliz h- Ash   T & M Sayer, St. Sidwell's EXETER

PEARLWARE TEA CANISTERS

A mould for one of the cherubs was found behind a wall at the site of the old Folly Pottery in 1992.

S.C. 1792   Sarah Ralph 1793
Sarah Hall   1793
Elizth. Taylor Born March 18th 1795

R.B. 1796	Saml. Harding 1796	Edgar Galliford 1796
D. Bickle Crediton 1796	Mary Southcott 1797	Ann Colridge 1797
T. Carpenter 1798	Mary Seaman 1798	Mary Podbury 1798
T. M. Harris 1798	Sarah Sheppard 1798	

VERSES INSCRIBED ON TEA CANISTERS

*Time how short,
Eternity how long,
Prepare to meet thy God.*

*My dear mother
When this you see
Remember me
Tho many miles
We distant be*

BOX (shaped as a cauliflower)
M. Stooke 1796

JUG
J & S. Gale 1818

PEARLWARE TEAPOTS
Betty Norris, SANDFORD 1793
Mary Neck, ILSINGTON 1809

Note the typical squiggles on each side of the date.

PEARLWARE INKWELLS

S.W. 1791   Thomas Tapper 1808
Samuel Norrish, Buckland in the Moor, 1814
William Norrish, Buckland in the Moor, 1814
Richard Willcocks, Bovey Tracey, 1815
Mary Mortimore, North Bovey Febry 29th 1816

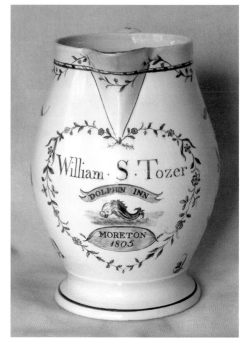

JUGS
W.M. BOVEY 1800.
Thos. Strong 1796

William S. Tozer, Dolphin Inn,
MORETON 1805

Rich d. Cockerman Treburley
LEZANT

William Ellis born. May. 6. 1812
CHAGFORD

JAR
A large blue painted jar is inscribed
"ANCHOVEY"

FLASK
W.P. Downing 1792
Grog is the Liquor of Life

COFFEE CAN
A Present for John

Slip Decoration

Simple slip decoration on creamware figures was a speciality of the Indeo Pottery in the late 18th Century.   Very few other potteries used the technique.

MARKS.   INDEO POTTERY 1766 - 1836

Almost all of the products of the Indeo Pottery were unmarked, but the following have been recorded, some only on sherds found at the factory site.

Scratched blue mark on a saltglaze tea canister made by Thomas Prouse, foreman of The Indeo Pottery.

Impressed pseudo-Chinese seal mark on engine turned glazed redware, particularly teapots, circa 1770 - 1790. A reverse version of this mark exists, but is not from Indeo.

Printed mark on pearlware showing pattern name - 1790s. This is the only known mark showing a pattern name (found on a sherd excavated at Indio).

Impressed marks on creamware of the 1790s.

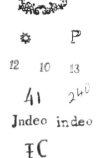

Painted and scratched marks, possibly test numbers.

Impressed marks on domestic ware of the 1790s.

Scratched initials, possibly of John Crane, who was working at Indeo in the 1790s.

The Folly Pottery

 new pottery was built in 1801 at Lord Courtenay's original works at Bovey Heathfield, *(the site now occupied by House of Marbles.)*

A letterhead showing the Folly Pottery in about 1820.

William Mead, a woolcomber, set up as a competitor to the Indeo Pottery in partnership with blacksmith Samuel Lamble. This new enterprise went through several partnership changes and by 1820, *"because of the failure of different speculators,"* had become known as, "The Folly Pottery."

John Pike Jones, curate of North Bovey, wrote of the workers, *"one could see the emaciated and paralytic potters dragging out a wretched existence,"* their state caused by poisoning from the raw lead glazes in use at that time.

This was one of the largest potteries in the West of England, employing up to fifty workers in virtually all pottery trades. Being so far from the centre of British pottery making and having most raw materials close by, it was convenient, if not necessary, to carry out all pottery processes within one enterprise. This was to distinguish Bovey Tracey from Staffordshire, where potters relied on specialist firms to provide such things as engravings, glazes and raw materials.

Two massive kilns were built, between them capable of holding 1600 saggars of ware. A narrow gauge tramway line was installed to transport Bovey coal from the lignite pit to the kilns. The Haytor Granite Company's granite railroad was built through The Pottery in about 1820 and was used for transporting goods to and from the Teignbridge Canal. The Honeychurch family took over in 1805, and continued the business until 1836 when, together with The Indeo Pottery, the business declined. Buildings of the original Folly Pottery are open to the public at House of Marbles.

PRODUCTS Very little is known of the products. J.P.Jones wrote of, *"A considerable quantity of blue and white earthenware, and a black ware in imitation of Wedgwood's."*

Excavations have revealed creamware, pearlware and blue printed pottery.

Top : *Pearlware plate with printed willow pattern border and inscription.   Betsy Hortop retired as schoolmistress at Lifton, Devon in 1840.*

Left: *White jug passed down through the family of Les Manley of Bovey Tracey, said to have been made by Honeychurch and Company.*

MARKS   There are no known marks for the Folly Pottery.

The Bovey Tracey Pottery Company

By 1827, both the Indeo and Folly Potteries were said to be, *"in a state of insolvency due to bad management,"* and soon fell into dereliction. The Honeychurches were declared bankrupt in 1835, but their Folly Pottery was not abandoned completely, being revived in 1843 by the partnership of John Divett of Yarner and his brother-in-law Captain Thomas Wentworth Buller (R.N.) under the name Buller, Divett and Company. The pottery was rented from the Earl of Devon's estate for £36 per annum in 1843, *"not less than £400,"* to be spent on erecting new buildings and a kiln.

A newspaper reported in 1845: *"the heath. is at times perfumed by the foul exhalations of a gigantic tiling and earthenware pottery, which casts its noxious vapours far and wide over the heath. The picture by F. Bedford, photographer to H.R.H. The Prince of Wales, shows the pottery in about 1890.*

Whites Directory of Devonshire for 1850 noted that the Company was making *"earthenware equal in quality and design to the best Staffordshire wares."* In 1851 there were three hundred employees, many of whom had migrated from The Potteries of that northern County.

Lignite continued in use as a fuel at The Bovey Tracey Pottery, but only for firing red bricks and tiles. Good quality coal had to be brought by sailboat to Teignmouth, along the Stover Canal to Teigngrace, and to the works by horse and cart, where it was used for high temperature firings of biscuit and glazed whiteware. The rapid introduction of railway systems offered a way of alleviating the high cost of transporting good coal to the Pottery. John Divett asked the people of Bovey Tracey to contribute to the cost of a new railway line, explaining that the alternative might be to close the Pottery. The South Devon Railway between Newton Abbot and Bovey Tracey was opened in 1866, part of it running along the course of the old granite railroad. The new line brought an influx of tourists in the summer months, made welcome at the pottery with conducted tours.

T.W. Buller had died by then, leaving his share of the business to his son Wentworth William Buller. They developed the manufacture of patent kiln furniture at Bovey Tracey, transferring to Hanley in Staffordshire in the 1860s , the beginnings of Bullers Limited, one of the world's foremost electrical insulator manufacturers. John Divett was said to have raised the Bovey Potteries to a successful position by the time he died in 1885. The Divett family continued the business, with a new manager, Mr. Clay from Staffordshire, but there was a steady decline.

In June 1891 the workers went on strike after their wages were cut by 20 per cent. Mr. Clay tried in vain to break the strike by importing workers from his native Stoke-on-Trent. By 1894 the pottery was bankrupt, yet again, and lay empty for 18 months.

PRODUCTS. Murray's Handbook of Devon for 1895 described the Bovey Tracey Pottery wares, *"The Bovey manufactures are white, printed and painted ware, besides ware of stained clay (drab, lilac etc.) The ordinary ware is very good, and the higher quality much above the average."*

This was a "Staffordshire" pottery in the Devon countryside, and many unmarked examples made here are attributed to that County as a generic description.

MESS WARE, *commissioned for use on ships of the Royal Navy. The Bovey Tracey Pottery was a major supplier. Patterns continued into the 20th Century, with the heads of the young Queen Victoria and of Edward VII.*

"THE GEM," pattern, probably first made in the 1840s. The pictures of country folk represent Spring, Summer, Autumn and Winter, but most pots do not include all four seasons.

Noted inscriptions:

DEVON ARMS
Teignmouth

George Inn Eascott
Hill SWINDON

A. E. Gater, China
Rooms, Exeter

PRESENTATION MUGS *The handle mouldings are distinctive to The Bovey Tracey Pottery Company. The incurved shape was continued well into the 20th Century.*

Noted inscriptions: Wesleyan Bazaar Bovey Tracey 1856
Laura Emily Pinsent, A Present from Bovey 1859
Charlotte E. Shinner Born at Ashburton, August 19th 1878

A selection of 19th Century Bovey Tracey Pottery.

OINTMENT POTS *Many of these pots, both glazed and unfinished, have been found at Bovey Tracey. They were made until 1902 and possibly later.* **Poor Mans Friend** *was a concoction for the treatment of burns and scalds, chilblains, sore eyes, pimples on the face, and scurvy, - made of lard, beeswax and lead by Beach and Barnicott of Bridport, Dorset .*

CLOTTED CREAM JARS   *These jars are often found in places other than Devon, sometimes in Victorian tips, having been sent up Country by rail for the delight and benefit of Victorian middle and upper classes. Clotted cream jars of various forms were a staple product of The Bovey Tracey potteries from the late 18th Century.*

Horner's Devonshire Clotted Cream
Horner's Cream Cheese can generally be procured where this is sold
Established 1836
Anyone using this jar for trade purposes will be prosecuted.
Devonshire Clotted Cream
For use with tarts, stewed fruits &c. It is unrivalled, and to Coffee, Cocoa and Chocolate it gives a richness and flavour unapproachable. Children and persons requiring a nutritive diet can by its free use greatly benefit, while as a rival to Cod liver oil, and in cases of debility and consumption, it is highly recommended and prescribed by the medical profession.
Entered at Stationers Hall

This inscription is one of several variations. The claimed beneficial effects of the product in the treatment of common ailments - consumption (tuberculosis) and debility, reflect the 19th Century concern for serious and common illnesses.

BEER AND CYDER MUGS

Mocha ware measuring jug, (an unglazed waster found locally); and a later mocha ware tavern mug.

Raised pad mark applied by the Bovey Tracey Pottery to tavern measures. Other potteries had different versions. These unauthorised marks were discontinued in 1878.

Verification mark applied by the local Inspector of Weights & Measures on tavern measures, from 1879. Etched by sandblasting through a stencil, these marks are not easily seen on the glaze.

.	VR	1879 - 1902	*Queen Victoria*
.	ER	1902 - 1910	*King Edward VII*
.	GR	1910 -	*King George V*

Each local authority had its own verification mark numbers, issued by The Board of Trade. Devon County numbers are the most likely to appear on Bovey Tracey tavern measures, sold by them as "Government Stamped," but a full list of local verification mark numbers is given:

81	South Molton	377	Barnstaple
87	Exeter City	440	Tiverton
149	Plymouth	583 - 588	Devon County
243	Totnes	Exon	Exeter City

MARKS: BOVEY TRACEY POTTERY COMPANY

1843 - 1894   It is likely that most early ware was not marked, perhaps not before about 1870.

Printed marks, some with pattern names:

Impressed marks, some with year numbers.

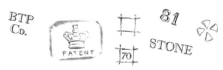

Printed mark for Hill and Teasdel, New Zealand, agents for the Bovey Tracey Pottery Company.

Printed mark for the ships' chandlers F. Primavesi and Sons, Cardiff, Swansea and Newport.   The backstamp was supplied by Primavesi, who were in business from 1850 as "and Son".   "and Sons," was substituted some time before 1881 and continued until 1915.

The Bovey Pottery Company Limited

everal hundred local workers and their families had become dependant on the Bovey Tracey Potteries and subsidiary businesses by the 1890s. The permanent closure of this major employer was averted when the directors of Pountney & Company's pottery at Bristol intervened, almost certainly at the instigation of Charles Davey Blake, the Devon ball clay supplier who was a major creditor of both potteries. The new Bovey Pottery Company was incorporated on 22nd December 1894 under the directorship of T.B. Johnston of Bristol.

The Bovey Pottery in the 1920s.

Strong investment in new buildings, equipment and pottery designs went on over many years and gave new impetus to trade. In 1916, "The Pottery Gazette" was able to report that The Bovey Pottery had become much more extensively known, having made "phenomenal headway," in bringing their products into line with more centrally located manufacturers. They were now producing pottery, *"that will meet the needs of the million,"* and were *"a powerful force,"* with a display at Frank Findlay, their London representative's showroom in Holborn. A 1927 report spoke of,

"sensible, useful, everyday wares, capable of interesting the man in the street, selling readily wherever durable ware at the lowest possible price consistent with quality is in demand. ...in Staffordshire generally described as 'second-grade' earthenware."

An increase in foreign competition and the General Strike of 1926 almost brought the pottery to a standstill. In 1928 they made a loss of £165; the biscuit and glost ovens were running at half their capacity. As with all industry and commerce, the depression of the 1930s caused even more problems and the Bovey Pottery was never to fully recover.

Many of the pottery workers were enlisted during World War II and those who remained concentrated on war work, making undecorated utility ware, much of it for the armed forces - something of a boost to local employment, the workforce increasing to 250, with greater use of female labour. A small amount of decorated ware was made for export from 1942.

The post war period saw some recovery, compared with the 1930s. There were 205 workers employed in 1950. New designs were introduced for the high class market, and the "Blue Waters" range for the novelty and holiday trade. There was also an attempt to cater for the new "contemporary" taste, but Government contracts still formed a substantial part of the business, 40 percent of the output being supplied to The Ministry of Works.

The economic climate of the mid 1950s dampened hopes for renewed prosperity at the pottery. Export orders were being lost, Harold MacMillan imposed his "credit squeeze," and purchase tax on crockery was increased to 30 percent. By 1956 the workforce was down to 135. To add to the economic pressures, the Clean Air Act of that year suddenly required that the coal fired bottle kilns, some of which were in any case showing signs of subsidence, be put out of use in favour of cleaner tunnel kilns.

The directors were forced to make some harsh decisions and a choice had to be made between their two potteries - to close either Bovey or Bristol (where they were based). They decided to recommend the closure of The Bovey Pottery, but before the necessary shareholders' meeting was held, they were approached by senior Bovey Pottery staff who suggested putting the facts to the potters. In mid-November 1956 the Bovey Pottery workers were persuaded to accept a reduction in wages of 1/6d in the pound. The wage cut was tempered by the directors agreeing to give up their profits, and the office staff accepting a 10 percent reduction in their salaries - and there was an unexpected benefit. Short time working had been introduced, but there was an increase in orders when the Sales Representative was able to offer Bovey Tracey pottery at lower prices. The workers suddenly had the prospect of a net increase in wages from overtime payments.

Three weeks later, Bill Tranter of The National Society of Pottery Workers, based in Stoke-on-Trent, travelled to Bovey Tracey, and on December 7th called his 84 members out on strike, virtually closing The Pottery. By 21st December the Company had announced that they were going into voluntary liquidation. The strike was called off by The Union in mid-January 1957, but it was too late and the industrial whiteware potteries of Bovey Tracey were brought to an end.

Several workers were kept on for a few months to complete outstanding orders and clear up the workshops. Ongoing contracts, and some stock and equipment was transferred to Bristol. Other stock was either scrapped or sold. Moulds destined for the Blue Waters tip were diverted to other local potteries.

A selection of 20th Century Bovey Pottery.

BADGED WARE. *A service for institutions and hotels. The plate is a traveller's sample showing badges for several Devon hotels. Examples from as far afield as Glasgow, London and Iran have been noted.*

ASHTRAYS ETC.

Note the swastika on the pre-war Carlsberg ashtray.

BLUE WATERS *A selection of novelty wares, named after Blue Waters flooded lignite pit near the pottery. Circa 1954 - 1957.*

DARTMOOR WARE AND FRUIT WARE

Fruit Ware was made in imitation of Scottish Wemyss Ware, and was introduced in 1916 as part of a trade war with Germany, where Villeroy and Boch were making similar products. Several other potteries made imitations of Wemyss Ware. Bovey Fruit Ware does not usually have a Bovey mark, but can be distinguished by its brushwork and a typical thin green line on its edge.

NURSERY RHYME SERIES AND NURSERY WARE.

Left: *Examples of lithographs (transfers), still on their backing papers, used from the 1930s to the 1950s on the Nursery Rhymes series. Standard Bovey Pottery marks were used. Other manufacturers used the same designs.*

Below: *Baby's Plate is an example of the* **Nursery Rhymes Series.** *The other two - Old Woman and Little Boy Blue - are from the* **Nursery Ware Series** *introduced in the early 1950s. See page 36 for the distinctive mark.*

COMMEMORATIVES

Many Bovey Pottery commemoratives are inscribed with local Devon town and village names. Standard pottery marks were normally used, although some were not marked.

The Edward VIII mug is inscribed " Coronation May 12ᵗʰ 1937." Rather than waste them on the King's abdication, many ready-made commemoratives were hurriedly overprinted in black.

OUR GANG A series of 19 Wartime characters marketed from October 1940 and still available in the 1950s.

The Big Three, first advertised in October 1945: *Churchill (The Boss, reintroduced), Roosevelt and Stalin.*

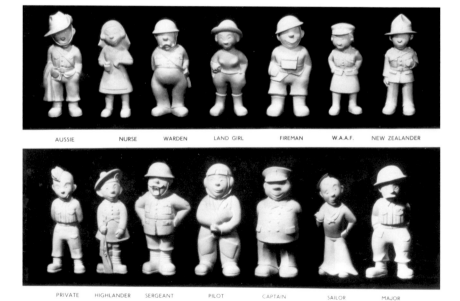

The first series was introduced in October 1940 and comprised 15 figures :

The Boss	*Aussie*	*Nurse*	*Warden*
Land Girl	*Fireman*	*W.A.A.F.*	*New Zealander*
Private	*Highlander*	*Sergeant*	*Pilot*
Captain	*Major*	*Sailor*	

Designed and modelled by Gwynneth Holt and Fenton Wyness, they were finished in a neutral smooth glaze. Coloured versions are likely to have been decorated after leaving the pottery.

Hit and Muss were introduced in March 1941 - the two rarest figures of the series.

BYRON PATTERN *printed with designs by B.M. Byron, circa 1955 - 57.*

MARKS: BOVEY POTTERY COMPANY LIMITED
1894 - 1957

Early printed marks, some with pattern names. 1894 - c.1930. Note that "Japonica" has no pottery name. "B.T.Co" appears to be an engraver's error. "B.P.Co" or "B.P.Co. Ltd" were generally used.

caution The initials BPCo and BPCoLtd were used by other potteries, notably Brownhills Pottery Company, Britannia Pottery Company and Blyth Porcelain Company. Other publications may attribute the marks incorrectly.

Scratched mark, noted on a plaque modelled with classical figures.

Impressed date marks showing the month and year of making. The ware may have been stored for some years as biscuit before being decorated and finished.

Impressed size mark in inches.

Free-hand painted marks on Dartmoor Ware and fruit ware (W) Circa 1916 - 1950.

Printed mark for,
McDowell's Sydney,
Australia.

Pre World War 2 marks, with "B"
added from about 1942.

Marks used from World War 2 onwards, "B" from c.1942 to 1952.

Standard printed mark c.1952 - 1957.

Printed crests and marks on wares made for H.M. Government.

Paper label and printed marks on factory samples. 1950s.

Printed mark for the high-class retailer Thomas Goode and Company, Mayfair, London W. and marks for other dealers, c. 1930 - 1957.

See also: Plichta, page 40

 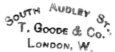

Novelties, fancies and commemoratives.

Blue Waters *(Page 28) c.1954 - 1957*
Our Gang, *(Pages 32) including the character name. 1940 - 1950s*
Nursery Ware *(Page 30) c.1952 - 1957, not to be confused with the Nursery Rhymes series, which had standard pottery marks*
Byron *(Page 33) c.1955 -1957.*
British Pottery Manufacturers Federation *on commemoratives (page 31) 1930s-1953.*

MADE IN ENGLAND

Wemyss Ware

emyss Ware originated in 1882 at The Fife Pottery in Scotland and was aimed at a high-class market. Freehand painted by skilled artists, it was a high quality decorative domestic earthenware developed from the white clay and colours previously used for making ordinary commercial pottery - painted with all manner of subjects from nature - flowers, fruits, cocks and hens and many more, in a bold and lifelike manner.

In 1930 The Bovey Pottery bought the Wemyss moulds and trade name from the defunct Fife Pottery. The head Wemyss Ware decorator, Joseph Nekola, moved to Bovey Tracey and continued this unique tradition until he died in 1952.

Examples of Bovey Pottery Wemyss Ware.

Changes in public taste meant that Bovey Wemyss Ware was never made in large amounts, going only to a small appreciative market. Wemyss Ware with the Wemyss mark was supplied by the Bovey Pottery direct to the trade and through their many worldwide agents.

The London agents for Wemyss Ware from 1930 to 1952 were Wallace and Frank Findlay of Holborn and Piccadilly. Wemyss Ware was continued until The Bovey Pottery closed in 1957, after which Pountney's Pottery at Bristol, who had co-directors with the Bovey Pottery and a joint share in the London showrooms, assumed the moulds and rights and attempted to make it, but with no success.

Several attempts were made to revive the tradition after 1957. In 1987, Wemyss Ware true to the original technical and artistic ideals was reintroduced as a result of a project initiated by H.R.H. The Prince of Wales. The new ware, made by the author of this book, is painted exclusively with original Wemyss underglaze colours and Wemyss freehand decorating techniques - each one individually. A few of the old Bovey Tracey moulds survive, and are used alongside new ones.

MARKS: WEMYSS WARE, 1930 - 1957

Handpainted underglaze marks. Pattern numbers 221 and 213 were from The Fife Pottery catalogue. Plichta marks were also used on Wemyss Ware (see page 40).

Wemyss.
Made in England.

Wemyss.
221

Wemyss.
Ware

Wemyss.
213.

Wemyss.

Wemyss

WEMYSS

WEMYSS WARE
R.H.&S.

Impressed marks on biscuit ware transferred from the Fife Pottery in 1930. Take care. Fakes and forgeries do exist.

Signatures of Wemyss decorators: Joseph Nekola, Esther Clark, Wanda Woloszczuk, Florrie Woollacott.

Nekola.
pinxt.

J. Nekola.

J.N.
April 1948.

E.C 1957

W W
F. W.

Other marks used by the Wemyss decorators.

Bovey
Walden
by J.N

"Wessex"
handpainted
made in
England

Moorland

Jazz

BOVEY
POTTERY
DEVON
ENGLAND

MADE IN
ENGLAND

Plichta

an Plichta, a London glass wholesaler, started buying pottery at Bovey Tracey in 1939, after Germany invaded his native Czechoslovakia and his main supply of imports ceased .

There is a considerable amount of confusion about Jan Plichta's role in the story of Wemyss ware. Incorrect second-hand verbal information supplied to an eminent researcher in the 1980s is often repeated in price guides and by experts. Persistent statements that Plichta made Wemyss Ware, was a decorator, or had the Wemyss agency or "rights" are nonsense. He appreciated the qualities of Wemyss Ware, but bought it with his own PLICHTA mark. Besides Wemyss Ware, The Bovey Pottery Company made lower quality painted and printed wares for Plichta - again with his preferred personal mark applied at The Bovey Pottery. He would often by-pass the office staff, sometimes to their annoyance, and deal directly with the Bovey Pottery decorators. There is no doubt that he brought a large amount of work to the Pottery in difficult economic times and he was well liked by the Bovey Tracey workers.

Jan Plichta also bought pottery from The Devon Tors Art Pottery, and from several other manufacturers, notably Mayer's Elton Pottery in Stoke-on-Trent, usually with the Plichta mark. The Elton Pottery also decorated some Bovey Pottery animals, but with overglaze enamels rather than with underglaze colours, which were used at Bovey. All Plichta pottery is relatively uncommon.

A selection of novelties made for Jan Plichta at The Bovey Pottery, including freehand painted, and handpainted wares.

MARKS: PLICHTA   These were applied underglaze at the Bovey Pottery.

Right: *Artist's name, Eric Bailey, on lithographs originally engraved for Plichta. Dates show the year of the original artwork.*

Below: *Printed marks used from the mid 1940s -
- 1956, and handpainted mark of the 1940s.
These marks were used on Wemyss Ware and
on cheaper lines.*

EricBailey 1941

ERIC BAILEY

PLICHTA LONDON ENGLAND	PLICHTA LONDON *Made in England*	PLICHTA LONDON ENGLAND HANDPAINTED	*MADE IN ENGLAND* *PLICHTA* *LONDON*

Similar marks were used on wares made by other potteries for Plichta. "Handpainted" novelties were in fact often handpainted over transfer prints.

The Other Potteries

his book is primarily concerned with the industrial potteries of Bovey Tracey based on Staffordshire traditions and which closed in 1957. It would not be complete, however, without a brief mention of other potteries established in the area.

THE BOVEY TRACEY ART POTTERY.

In the early 1920s Enoch Staddon, owner of The Torquay Pottery at Hele Cross, opened The Bovey Tracey Art Pottery opposite the big Bovey Pottery. Vincent Arthur Kane and his wife Marjorie Kane (daughter of Enoch Staddon) managed the pottery at first and eventually owned it. They made red clay art ware, much of it slip decorated, a favourite design being blue scroll on white. Small animals were also made.

Vincent Kane outside the pottery in the mid 1930s

Marks   Circa 1920 to c. 1942:   Variations of "Bovey Tracey" or "Bovey Tracey Art Pottery" were used, often scratched.

DEVONMOOR ART POTTERY

Established at Liverton in 1913, but closed in 1914, - re-opened in 1922, when a bottle kiln was transferred from Candy and Company. The kiln is still to be seen. Novelty and art wares were made including "Blue of Devon." The pottery is well known for its range of Toby jugs and small cottages.

   Marks   1922 - 1970s :   Variations of DEVONMOOR. Some wares are only marked with decorators' initials.

DEVON TORS ART POTTERY COMPANY

In 1921, brothers William and Frank Bond opened their pottery opposite The Bovey Pottery, at which they had both previously worked. Being so near the big Pottery, they made no attempt to compete, and made tourist and art ware in the Torquay style, all in a brown clay body. Some employees worked at both potteries, splitting their time between the two. Many pots were unmarked, as they were to be sold at holiday towns other than Bovey Tracey. The clay was originally brought from Watcombe, but 80 tons was acquired free for the taking from a building site near Torquay.

Marks : Devon Tors
1921-1967
Printed marks

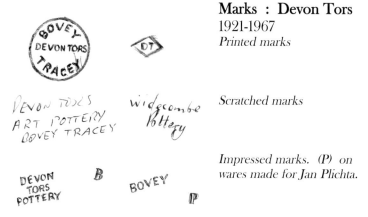

Scratched marks

Impressed marks. (P) on wares made for Jan Plichta.

WIDECOMBE POTTERY The mark occurs on pottery brought in by the Middleweek family for sale in their shop at Widecombe-in-the-Moor. The pottery was supplied from Stoke-on-Trent, by Devon Tors, and by Will Young of the Runnaford Pottery, Devon.

Widecombe Pottery marks were applied according to the styles of the potters :

DEVONSHIRE POTTERIES LIMITED

The Devonshire Pottery was established in around 1947 in the buildings previously occupied by The Bovey Tracey Art Pottery. Besides their own name, they also used the Trentham Art Ware mark, which was incorporated to the wholesalers G. Hardy and Company Limited of Nottingham and later of Mitcham, Surrey, who had an interest in The Devonshire Pottery. They produced pottery animals, novelties and kitchenware; mainly in a white clay body, but some in brown with slip decoration. The pottery closed on 30th April 1982.

Marks : Devonshire Potteries Limited   1947 - 1982.

Printed marks

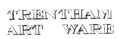

Trentham Art Ware marks were used from 1959.
Left : Removable Paper label
Right : Impressed (moulded) mark.

DEVON   Ʊ5Ʊ

Left :   *Mark scratched through black slip.*
Right :   *Impressed mould number.*

CANDY AND COMPANY LIMITED 1882 - 1963
Great Western Potteries, Chudleigh

The beaker and inkwell on the brick are "Chudleigh Ware," of the 1880s. The ashtray and flower vase were made later and have "Candy" marks.

Established by Frank Candy, possibly as early as 1875. Initially the pottery was made from clay extracted from a large deposit adjoining the site. Early wares were of vitrified stoneware, mostly bricks and ornamental architectural ceramics. In the 1880s a small amount of art pottery resembling the products of Doulton and Company of Lambeth, and known as "Chudleigh Ware," was made. An Art Ware department was established in 1916 and a new range of Wescontree Art ware was made from 1922 to 1957. The site is still in use as a tileworks.

MARKS : Great Western Pottery (Candy)

Impressed and scratched marks for the GREAT WESTERN POTTERY CHUDLEIGH, (1880s), including decorator's initials. The X mark is impressed.

Left: Embossed marks, sometimes including the shape number. 1922 - circa 1926.

Left: Printed marks, c.1925 - 1940.

Left: Metal foil stick-on label, c. 1930 - 1940.
Right: Printed mark, c. 1947 - 1957

House of Marbles and The Bovey Pottery

After 1957 the Bovey Pottery site was owned by Wyatt and Bruce Limited who, besides carrying on their agricultural feed business, let several of the old pottery buildings to a succession of businesses - motor engineers and a battery hen farmer amongst others.

House of Marbles acquired the site for the manufacture of their games and glassware in 1990. Their interest in the history of the Bovey Pottery sparked an attempt to resurrect pottery making on the site. The Bovey Pottery name was re-registered and a small group of potters produced a new version of Dartmoor Ware in the style of the 1930s. They also made moneyboxes and animals under the new Bovey Pottery mark. After six years without profit the management shut down the new pottery, finally deciding that they should concentrate on glass and games - industries which they understood best.

MARKS : Bovey Pottery Company Limited 1994-99

Printed and handpainted marks, including painters' names and initials.

The Bovey Tracey Pottery Museum

There has been a national interest in the history of the Bovey Tracey Potteries since 1970, when Norman Stretton, F.S.A., presented new research on the Indeo Pottery to the English Ceramics Circle.

In 1988, I began research into the history of the later Bovey Pottery Company after being asked to make Wemyss Ware as part of a project initiated by H.R.H. The Prince of Wales. Even with the national scholarly interest, many collectors had never heard of The Bovey Tracey Potteries. This was remedied to a large extent when House of Marbles opened their glassmaking and toy business in the old pottery buildings in 1990, and turned a substantial part of it into a museum - glass and marbles of course, and pottery. Many people came forward with new information. Some had worked at the old Bovey potteries; others had been quietly collecting or preserving the artefacts and history. Excavations of local sites by volunteers have rescued a considerable quantity of archaeological material

The Museum is now a focal point for the growing number of people, specialists as well as those with a more general interest, who seek information on the local potteries and their 250 year history. It is open to the public, free of charge, between 9 a.m. and 5 p.m. on most days of the year.

Brian Adams

Glossary

A s well as providing technical explanations for those who are not acquainted with pottery making, this serves as a guide to some of the kinds of pottery made at Bovey Tracey.

Ball Clay   Plastic sedimentary clay. The Bovey Basin is one of the world's most important sources of ball clay, so called because it was cut from the ground in cubes, which became more rounded as they were handled in transit.

Creamware   White earthenware of creamy colour, developed by Josiah Wedgwood and his 18th Century contemporaries. Also known as "Queen's Ware," in honour of Queen Charlotte. Creamware superseded saltglaze at Indeo in 1771.

Engine turned ware   Pottery on which decorative fluting and ridges are formed by turning the raw pot on an oscillating rose engine lathe, an expensive piece of equipment in any pottery. It was made at Indeo in the 18th Century.

Lignite (known locally as Bovey Coal)   Soft brown coal in a state of formation between its woody origins and true coal. The heat given off on burning is about one fifth that of hard coal. Lignite is stratified with ball clay in the Bovey Basin.

Mocha Ware   Pottery on which a fernlike decoration is formed by applying an acidic colour to wet alkaline slip. It has a similarity with Mocha stone from Arabia.

Pearlware   A variety of creamware on which a blue tinted glaze was used to imitate Chinese porcelain.

Porcelain   A vitreous translucent ceramic, more or less white in colour. Several kinds were made at Indeo for a short time in the 18th Century. Small quantities of bone china were brought in and decorated at the Bovey Pottery in the 20th Century.

Saggar   A fired clay box in which pottery was protected from direct flame and kiln ash during firing in a bottle kiln. The word is a corruption of "safeguard." Local dialect was "zegger."

Saltglaze   (1) A term applied to thinly potted white saltglazed ware made in the 18th Century as a substitute for imported Chinese porcelain. (2) A glaze formed by the chemical action of vaporised salt on a clay surface. Common salt was thrown into the kiln at the height of its firing.

Sherds   Broken pottery pieces, so common locally that they were known as "landsherds." It is said that a favourite game of a few mischievous people of Bovey Tracey was to throw landsherds at the inhabitants' front doors and run away.

Slip   A liquid clay and water mix, used for casting and for decorating pottery.

Sparkle Pottery   A type of slip decorated pottery which shimmers with a sparkle in strong light. It was first discovered in local excavations. The few rare examples so far found in collections can almost all be attributed to the Bovey Tracey Potteries of the early 1800s.

Potteries in The Land of Clay

Map labels: Topsham, HALDON, DARTMOOR, Bovey Tracey, Bovey Pottery, Fore St, Indeo, Devon Tors, Bovey Tracey Art Pottery, Chudleigh, Ashcombe, Exon Art Pottery, BALL CLAY BEDS, BOVEY HEATHFIELD, Candy, Heathfield, Dawlish, Devonmoor, Liverton, Kingsteignton, Ashburton, Teignmouth, Buckfastleigh, Newton Abbot, Aller Vale, Kingskerswell, Longpark, Watcombe, Hele Cross, Torquay

KEY
Railways
The important potteries
Significant places
Clay workings
Pottery sites

0   5   10
Scale of miles